EAGLE HILLS EAGLE RIDGE EAGLE LANDING

Brett Neveu

BROADWAY PLAY PUBLISHING INC
New York
www.broadwayplaypublishing.com
info@broadwayplaypublishing.com

EAGLE HILLS, EAGLE RIDGE, EAGLE LANDING
© Copyright 2007 by Brett Neveu

Cover art by Rich Sparks
First printing: September 2007
I S B N: 978-0-88145-351-5
Book design: Marie Donovan
Word processing: Microsoft Word
Typographic controls: Ventura Publisher
Typeface: Palatino
Printed and bound in the U S A

EAGLE HILLS, EAGLE RIDGE, EAGLE LANDING
was first presented by The Factory Theater in Chicago,
IL, from 12 July-17 August 2002. The cast and creative
contributors were:

KEVIN .... Dale Rivera
ANDY .... Keith Ellis
MIKE .... Peter Marcy

Director .... Steve Walker
Set design .... Darryl Miller
Lighting design .... Geoff Vines
Stage management .... William Sanders

EAGLE HILLS, EAGLE RIDGE, EAGLE LANDING
was subsequently presented by Spring Theatreworks
(produced by Jeffrey Horne) in New York, NY from
15 April-7 May 2002. The cast and creative contributors
were:

KEVIN .... Matthew Gray
ANDY .... Michael Brandt
MIKE .... Doug Simpson

Director .... Ian Morgan
Lighting design .... Justin Anderson
Stage management .... Emily Rems

SPECIAL THANKS

Ed Sobel, Ann Filmer, Ian Morgan, Russ Tutterow, Chicago Dramatists, AROT, Jonathan Lomma, and Chicago storefront theater.

CHARACTERS

MIKE
KEVIN
ANDY

all men in their early to mid-thirties

Time: present

Place: a bar in the suburb of a midwestern city

Production note: If no act break is taken, the last half of the song Foreplay *and the first part of the song* Long Time, *both by the band Boston, should play while the actors ready themselves for the next act. If an act break is taken, an extended version of* Foreplay / Long Time *may be used.*

to Kristen and Lia Pearl

ACT ONE

(Lights up. KEVIN *and* MIKE *sit at a table at a bar.)*

MIKE: There were these two women, and they were upset about something, so one of the women challenges the other woman to a duel. This was down in Missouri or something. The woman challenges the other woman, and the other woman accepts. The two ladies set a day, wait, then the day comes around. They both get up early in the morning, stand in some vacant lot, and shoot and kill each other. The two of them stood across from each other and killed each other right there. It wasn't even over anything important. They were both dead.

KEVIN: When was this?

MIKE: A month ago I think.

KEVIN: Where did you hear this?

MIKE: It's crazy that they killed each other, but I probably think it's a good thing, too.

KEVIN: It's good?

MIKE: I like it when things even out.

KEVIN: It evened out?

MIKE: One of these women was right and one of them was wrong. Instead of either one having to figure something out, or holding grudges against each other for a long time, the two of them shot each other instead.

It was quick answer to something that would have had brought up future problems.

KEVIN: The duel itself didn't create problems?

MIKE: It did, but then there it was all wrapped up. They killed each other. Everything balanced.

KEVIN: That's not balance.

MIKE: It's not?

KEVIN: With balance you have no consequences.

MIKE: Maybe it's not perfect balance.

KEVIN: It can't be imperfect balance and balance at the same time. It has to be either one or the other.

MIKE: I also heard this: "Sleep is the new sex."

KEVIN: Someone said that?

MIKE: I guess we want new things, and so we forget about sleep.

KEVIN: What you're saying is that what we've lost, we've found again, and because we've found it again, it's new.

MIKE: Yep.

KEVIN: Maybe the dueling ladies should have gotten more sleep.

MIKE: I don't think they're talking about *more* sleep. Just sleep.

KEVIN: Any sleep?

MIKE: I guess.

KEVIN: Like any sex.

MIKE: I think like any sex *used* to be.

KEVIN: So instead of having sex, you sleep instead?

MIKE: The sex is less often so that people would rather have sleep instead of sex. Everything's balanced again.

KEVIN: How is this balance if you are preferring one thing over the other?

MIKE: Everybody sleeps. And everyone should make quick decisions.

KEVIN: And that's balance?

MIKE: Yep.

KEVIN: Sleeping and dueling.

MIKE: Those are just things I heard.

KEVIN: I need another beer.

MIKE: I'll get it. What do you want?

KEVIN: It doesn't matter.

MIKE: Okay. Is anything else going on?

KEVIN: Not really.

MIKE: I think it's probably because everyone's tired that sleeping feels great. I guess that's my point.

KEVIN: I'm not tired.

MIKE: Maybe it's not tired, like sleeping tired. *(Pause)* I don't know what I'm talking about. I don't know. You want another beer?

KEVIN: Okay.

(MIKE exits towards the bar. KEVIN sits alone for a few moments. ANDY enters.)

ANDY: Is Mike at the bar?

KEVIN: Uh-huh.

(ANDY exits towards the bar. KEVIN sits alone for a few beats.)

(ANDY *and* MIKE *enter.* MIKE *carries two beers,*
ANDY *has one. They sit at the table.*)

ANDY: Are you guys hungry?

MIKE: Do you guys want some pretzels or something?

ANDY: I'll get some pretzels. (*He exits towards bar.*)

MIKE: I used to go to this other place back at my other
job and they'd have mustard for their pretzels.

KEVIN: They have mustard here.

MIKE: They had different mustard, like a Dijon mustard
or a spicy mustard. The kind here is hotdog mustard.

KEVIN: Then don't eat it.

MIKE: One time when I was here I was getting some
mustard and I had one of those little cups that you
squirt the mustard into, and the cup had some gum in it.

KEVIN: Gum?

MIKE: Somebody put their chewed gum in a mustard
cup. I'm glad that I hadn't put some mustard in that
cup and then dipped a pretzel into the mustard, then
ate the pretzel. I would have never known about the
gum until it was too late and I would have eaten all
the mustard before I would have noticed that there
was gum in the bottom of the cup.

KEVIN: You wouldn't have realized earlier that there
was a chunk of gum at the bottom of the cup?

MIKE: Maybe.

KEVIN: You would've noticed that something was in
there.

MIKE: Maybe.

(ANDY *enters with a basket of pretzels and some cups of
mustard.*)

MIKE: Did you look in those cups before you put mustard in them?

ANDY: For chewed gum?

MIKE: I told you about that?

ANDY: I can't believe someone did that!

MIKE: I was just saying that it was a good thing that I noticed it.

ANDY: Oh yeah.

MIKE: I would have never known that there was gum was in there.

KEVIN: If you hadn't noticed it, then you'd have never known, and it wouldn't have mattered.

MIKE: I would have realized what had happened, and then I would have gotten sick.

KEVIN: How would you have realized?

MIKE: Maybe when I threw it away or something.

KEVIN: What if you didn't notice at all?

ANDY: I think it's just weird that someone would do that.

MIKE: It's pretty funny.

ANDY: When did you guys get here?

MIKE: We just got here.

ANDY: There was a fire at my office today.

MIKE: A fire?

ANDY: The office kitchen caught on fire.

MIKE: It did?

ANDY: The microwave caught on fire.

MIKE: Something in the microwave caught on fire?

ANDY: It was weird, because nobody was cooking anything. It just caught on fire.

MIKE: Was it the wiring?

ANDY: We were all working and then the microwave just was on fire.

MIKE: Did someone put it out?

ANDY: It went out by itself.

KEVIN: You just let the fire burn itself out?

ANDY: It only lasted a second or two, then it was out.

MIKE: It was only on fire for a second?

ANDY: Maybe a couple of seconds.

KEVIN: That's not really a fire.

ANDY: It was on fire. That's a fire.

KEVIN: It was just a short or a flame up or something.

MIKE: Unless it was some strange fire that was really big and then suddenly it went out like it didn't happen in the first place.

ANDY: It was a small fire.

MIKE: Can you still use the microwave?

ANDY: No one uses it anyway.

KEVIN: Who saw the fire?

ANDY: We all saw it.

KEVIN: Everyone at your office was in the kitchen?

ANDY: No.

KEVIN: Then what do you mean?

ANDY: By what?

KEVIN: What do you mean you all saw it?

ANDY: We all saw the fire.

KEVIN: Everyone?

ANDY: No.

KEVIN: Then what do you mean?

ANDY: It was a small fire. The microwave caught on fire slightly.

KEVIN: I saw a fire on the news last night.

MIKE: You did?

KEVIN: They couldn't contain it. They had thousands of firefighters and it worked out that the fire was so big that it they had only one firefighter per square mile, that's how much of the forest was on fire.

ANDY: Where was it?

KEVIN: It was in a forest out west.

MIKE: My brother-in-law is a fireman.

KEVIN: These guys out west had to watch as a wall of flame nearly a mile high tore through the woods. They tried to contain it, but nothing they did worked.

MIKE: How long did the fire last?

KEVIN: Months.

ANDY: Months?

KEVIN: It burned nearly the whole forest down.

ANDY: It went on for months?

KEVIN: There were a lot of trees that caught fire.

ANDY: Months?

MIKE: That's a shame.

ANDY: (To KEVIN) Did you look up in Eagle Ridge on Sunday?

KEVIN: Laura's been up there, she looked at a few places. We drove around there last weekend.

ANDY: You drove around?

KEVIN: We've been looking.

ANDY: There's lots over near the bottom of the east subdivision, and the one right below Gary Heideman's place.

KEVIN: We drove by those.

ANDY: You missed seeing those others. There's more to see out there.

KEVIN: That's all right.

ANDY: If you would have looked at those others, I would have been able to look right past the slope from the back of my place and seen your deck.

MIKE: I can nearly see Andy's deck from my place.

KEVIN: We're still looking around.

MIKE: Those east lots have less trees.

ANDY: Up on that hill past Myer's it sort of flattens out. Where are you looking?

KEVIN: Laura's just been driving around and we're talking about a few of the lots.

MIKE: I was driving past one of those lots just south of the east lots and I think they're putting the transformer boxes over there.

ANDY: Those lots back up nearly to The Beltline. Cars go up and down that road all the time.

MIKE: Some people don't mind transformers on their property.

ANDY: They let the back of those lots just end out in that creek. It gets muddy back there.

MIKE: Some people like lots that end in the creek.

KEVIN: I think Laura's looking near the end of the east lot.

ANDY: They're adding onto the back of the street where you are now, aren't they?

KEVIN: A block past the end of our street.

ANDY: Are they extending Eagle Hills into the area just north of there?

KEVIN: They've lengthened the road about two blocks down.

ANDY: They're putting new streets just down there now?

KEVIN: They've extended it past us two blocks.

ANDY: I think there's a guy at my work that's moving into Eagle Hills next spring.

KEVIN: Oh.

ANDY: That area's getting pretty big over there. All you'll be able to see soon are the backs of your neighbor's houses. If you'd got that lot just west of us in Eagle Ridge you'd back up right into those trees. In the summer, it'd be like a fence.

MIKE: Birds come in the spring. It's great.

(Pause)

ANDY: What else?

KEVIN: Mike says sleep is the new sex.

ANDY: Okay.

MIKE: I just heard that somewhere.

ANDY: I can believe that.

KEVIN: And he was talking about some women that were in a duel.

ANDY: Oh right.

KEVIN: He was going into some whole "everything's balanced" thing.

ANDY: What thing?

MIKE: I don't know. Nothing.

ANDY: A balance thing?

KEVIN: *(To* MIKE*)* What were you talking about?

MIKE: I was talking about how things even out. Isn't that what I was talking about?

ANDY: What things evening out?

MIKE: I was saying that when things even out in the end, it's a good thing.

ANDY: And what did it have to do with the duel story?

MIKE: I don't want to get into this whole thing again.

KEVIN: Go ahead and explain it.

MIKE: No, no.

KEVIN: He was saying how things are the same.

MIKE: I was saying that when things are the same, things are better.

ANDY: Things are better when things are the same.

KEVIN: What things?

ANDY: Things are better when everything's equal.

KEVIN: When what's equal?

ANDY: Everything.

KEVIN: Everyone should be the same?

ANDY: Not everyone. Everything.

KEVIN: People should get everything equally?

ANDY: People who are the same should have the same things equally.

KEVIN: What if someone has better things?

ANDY: No one can have better things, because everything is equally available to everyone, as long as those people are the same.

KEVIN: Everything is equally available to everyone?

ANDY: It all depends on who you are the same as.

MIKE: I saw on T V those wild vacations down in the Caribbean.

ANDY: Wild vacations?

MIKE: It was about the wild places you could go if you were on a vacation in the Caribbean.

ANDY: What wild places?

MIKE: There were topless women everywhere. It looked like everyone was into whatever goes on down there. Everyone was drinking and having a great time.

ANDY: I think I've seen that show.

MIKE: It was a great show.

ANDY: Is it the show where they travel all over the world checking out the crazy places people go?

MIKE: It's probably the same one I'm talking about.

ANDY: I saw one where people went waterskiing.

MIKE: Where?

ANDY: On some island down south.

KEVIN: They went waterskiing?

ANDY: Parasailing, waterskiing, jetskiing.

KEVIN: You can do that around here.

ANDY: Not parasailing.

KEVIN: You can go waterskiing.

ANDY: That's the fun of it though, being able to have lots of choices.

KEVIN: I wouldn't choose parasailing.

ANDY: You should try it.

KEVIN: You've done it?

ANDY: No, but it looks like fun.

MIKE: What do you do? Parachute?

ANDY: You wear a parachute and someone pulls you around in a boat.

MIKE: How far up do you go?

ANDY: Pretty far.

MIKE: Then you come back down in the water?

ANDY: I don't know.

KEVIN: I think you come back down on the ground. If you landed in the water, you'd get all tangled up in the parachute and drown.

ANDY: You wouldn't drown.

KEVIN: What if you were up there and you got caught in a wind gust and you fell in the water and drowned?

ANDY: I don't think you'd drown.

KEVIN: What if the engine on the boat stopped working and then you fell into the water?

ANDY: They have all sorts of precautions, I'm sure.

KEVIN: But anything can happen.

MIKE: They should have T V shows like that, where they show you the fun times and then they show you the danger that happens, too.

ANDY: They have shows like that already.

MIKE: What shows are like that?

ANDY: I've seen shows like that.

KEVIN: What if you were parasailing and you got tangled up in the parachute while you were in the air, then the boat couldn't stop to help you, because if they did, you'd drown for sure, and if they put you over land, you'd break every bone in your body because you had no way of landing safely.

ANDY: You're adding all sorts of danger to something that isn't that dangerous.

KEVIN: Danger's the reason people parasail in the first place.

ANDY: There are all sorts of safety measures that you have to learn before you try.

MIKE: They don't show any safety stuff on those shows. They just show the people having fun doing whatever they want. I guess I've seen some shows that have people that talk about being hurt while doing crazy things on vacation, like a talk show with those people as guests. They have shows where the people sit around and talk to the victims of vacation accidents. Nobody ever looks hurt, but they say they were victims of these vacations, like they fell or were cut or something. But mostly they just have those shows where people are having a great time and drinking shots out of each other's belly buttons.

ANDY: I saw one where they drank a shot out of someone's bra. They held out this bra and drank out of it really fast.

MIKE: Sometimes they go too far on those shows.

ANDY: That was a little over the top.

KEVIN: I don't know what I'd do on one of those trips.

MIKE: That's why they have those shows.

KEVIN: I'd get lost going to buy a juice.

ANDY: You'd get lost?

KEVIN: Something like that.

ANDY: How would you get lost?

KEVIN: I'd take a wrong turn and end up somewhere.

ANDY: They make it incredibly easy to get around on those islands.

KEVIN: I know something would happen.

ANDY: This guy at my work went to one of those islands and he said he had a great time.

MIKE: Which island did he go to?

ANDY: I don't remember if it was an island. Maybe it was some southern coast region or something. But he had a great time. He got lots of sun and played golf.

MIKE: He played golf? Where?

ANDY: He said it was a beautiful course along the ocean.

MIKE: Which course was it?

ANDY: It was in Mexico, I think.

MIKE: I've never played golf in Mexico.

ANDY: From what this guy was saying, it was a great course.

KEVIN: He was in Mexico?

ANDY: I think that's what he said.

KEVIN: There must have been other stuff to do besides golf.

MIKE: I think it's fun to find different courses to play.

ANDY: I think it's a good way to meet people.

KEVIN: I'd do something else if I went down there.

ANDY: You should go down there.

KEVIN: I don't know what I'd do when I got there.

ANDY: It would depend where you went in Mexico. You could go to the Yucatan.

MIKE: Cancun?

ANDY: Cancun is in the Yucatan.

MIKE: I saw folks on that show go to Cancun. It looked like a great time.

ANDY: I'm sure they have all sorts of resorts down there. You should find one of those all-inclusive packages.

MIKE: Those are good. You don't even have to tip.

ANDY: I can ask that guy where he went.

KEVIN: That's okay.

ANDY: You don't want me to ask him about it?

KEVIN: I can call a travel agent or something.

ANDY: You don't need to do that. This guy has all that information already. He might even have some deal that some travel agent might not know about.

KEVIN: I'll take care of it.

ANDY: You don't want to go to Mexico?

KEVIN: I'm going to look into it.

ANDY: It's no trouble, I can ask that guy.

KEVIN: I want to see what other places I could go to in Mexico.

MIKE: Laura too, right? That'd be a wild time if you went down there without Laura.

KEVIN: Both of us would go.

MIKE: You should check the calendar at work tomorrow and see what vacation time is available. Gary Huffien is taking three weeks in May.

KEVIN: I don't even know if I'm going to Mexico.

MIKE: I always check the calendar and see what's available before I even think about any vacation.

ANDY: You check it even if you know no one is taking any vacation the same time you are?

MIKE: I don't know that until I check the calendar.

ANDY: What I'm saying is that what if you've decided to take a vacation and then you write down those days, not even thinking if someone had taken them off yet.

MIKE: What do you mean?

ANDY: Don't you just write down vacation days?

MIKE: I check the calendar first, then go from there.

ANDY: Why?

MIKE: I don't want to not get the days off I want.

ANDY: You should just take the days you want.

MIKE: I do.

ANDY: Without looking at the calendar first.

MIKE: That's the only way I can do it without it being all screwed up.

ANDY: You guys work at a weird place.

MIKE: It's not weird to try to get what you want.

ANDY: I'm saying that you aren't getting what you want. You're getting what's left over.

KEVIN: It's not usually as stressful it sounds to try and get time off .

MIKE: I'm not saying it's stressful.

KEVIN: Usually the days get approved.

ANDY: You have to get approval?

MIKE: Yes.

ANDY: It works different at my office.

KEVIN: You can just leave when you want and come back when you want?

ANDY: No. We have to submit the days off.

MIKE: You have to submit them?

ANDY: Then we find out if those days work.

KEVIN: It's the same thing we do.

ANDY: No, we have to just let management know when we're going to be gone.

MIKE: It's the same thing.

ANDY: I don't have to look at a calendar and try to work around anyone else's schedule. I just let them know when I'm going and when I'm coming back.

KEVIN: Then why do you have to submit your days?

ANDY: I guess I didn't mean "submit". I mean "let know".

KEVIN: It's the same thing.

ANDY: It's different.

KEVIN: It's the same.

ANDY: My company doesn't make me play games or make me feel like I need to walk carefully in order to get the vacation days I want. They never say I can't take certain days off.

MIKE: I always get the days off I want, too.

ANDY: Mine gives the employee more freedom.

KEVIN: I'm not taking any time off for a few months, anyway.

MIKE: That'll give you plenty of time to figure out where in Mexico you want to go.

ANDY: Monte Gause just got back from Hawaii.

MIKE: Hawaii. That'd be great.

ANDY: He says stay away from the big island.

MIKE: I heard that before.

KEVIN: I don't know where or when we'll go on vacation, but we'll go sometime.

ANDY: *(To* KEVIN*)* Have you ever been up to Monte Gause's house?

KEVIN: No.

ANDY: His house in Eagle Landing?

KEVIN: No.

MIKE: The lots in Eagle Landing are like double lots, compared to other lots.

ANDY: He converted his basement into a entertainment area, with a stereo and a television.

MIKE: Does he have a large screen T V?

ANDY: It's pretty big.

MIKE: I would love something like that.

ANDY: I'll probably do that when I have enough room.

KEVIN: What were you doing over at Monte Gause's?

ANDY: I was over there for dinner.

KEVIN: When was that?

ANDY: A couple of weeks ago.

MIKE: I bet he has a great view out of the back of that place.

ANDY: I looked out of the back and you could see right down over past Burnett's and over to 54.

MIKE: What's the deck like?

ANDY: He's got it so that it stretches around the side so you can get to the deck through the master bedroom.

MIKE: I love that property.

ANDY: He really lucked out. But he knows Bill Albee, and he's friends with Dave Herbolt.

KEVIN: What'd you talk about at dinner?

ANDY: Nothing really. We just talked and laughed. His wife is great.

MIKE: He has two kids.

ANDY: They were over at his wife's folk's.

KEVIN: Is he offering you a job?

ANDY: That's not why I was there.

MIKE: He offered you a job?

ANDY: No.

MIKE: That would be amazing.

KEVIN: Why were you over at his house?

ANDY: We saw each other at breakfast a while ago and he invited Susan and I over for dinner.

MIKE: There's still lots in Eagle Landing. We drove around there last week and there are about seven or eight still available.

ANDY: You were looking at lots?

MIKE: We were just driving around.

ANDY: You just moved to Eagle Ridge.

MIKE: We're not moving.

ANDY: Monte Gause went to Waikiki.

MIKE: How long was he there?

ANDY: A month.

MIKE: He went on a month vacation? If it were me, I wouldn't be able to go back to work after being gone a month.

ANDY: He came back and he was pretty tan.

MIKE: He stayed in a hotel for a month? That would be expensive to stay that long in a hotel.

ANDY: He rented a house. He put his family up in this house on the beach. He said it was amazing. They had a beautiful sunset every night. Except when it rained, then they stayed indoors and played cards.

MIKE: That's the way to do it.

ANDY: He showed us a few pictures of their trip. Most of the pictures were of their beach.

MIKE: Did it look warm?

ANDY: Yes.

KEVIN: Maybe I should do something like that.

ANDY: Monte said that it cost him quite a bit, but it was worth it to take the family on a trip they wouldn't forget.

KEVIN: If it were just Laura and I, it wouldn't cost that much.

MIKE: How are you going to get a month off from work? You can't be gone a month straight.

KEVIN: Not a month.

ANDY: Maybe you could go for a week, but that's pushing it.

MIKE: You could plan it for six months from now, then you could research it and find the best cost for everything.

ANDY: Make sure you don't go to the big island.

MIKE: Honolulu?

ANDY: The big island.

MIKE: Honolulu? *(Pause)* What kind of food do they eat in Hawaii?

ANDY: Fruit and ham.

MIKE: I don't think I've had any Hawaiian food.

ANDY: I had some guava jelly once.

KEVIN: That's not Hawaiian.

MIKE: Pineapple?

KEVIN: That's Hawaiian.

MIKE: That's why people put pineapple on hams.

KEVIN: What is why people put pineapple on hams?

MIKE: Andy said that Hawaiian food is fruit and ham.

ANDY: It's a garnish.

MIKE: I eat it.

ANDY: You can eat it.

MIKE: I like how it soaks up the ham flavor.

KEVIN: Does anyone need a beer?

ANDY: I'll get us some beer. What are we drinking?

MIKE: Anything's fine.

ANDY: Okay. *(He exits, taking the empty glasses from the table.)*

KEVIN: Why was Andy at Monte Gause's house?

MIKE: They're friends. *(Pause)* If Andy gets a job over there, we're right behind him.

KEVIN: Monte Gause is hiring him?

MIKE: They're friends.

KEVIN: I'm friends with Monte Gause.

MIKE: You are?

KEVIN: I've talked to him a few times.

MIKE: I've talked to him, too.

KEVIN: He's a little wacky.

MIKE: Really?

KEVIN: Don't you think so?

MIKE: No.

KEVIN: He tells jokes and takes vacations in Amsterdam.

MIKE: You don't like Amsterdam?

KEVIN: Do you like Amsterdam?

MIKE: I've never thought about it.

KEVIN: Do you like it?

MIKE: Probably.

(ANDY enters with three beers.)

MIKE: Kevin's saying Monte Gause is wacky.

ANDY: He's not wacky.

KEVIN: I didn't mean wacky.

ANDY: He's not wacky at all.

KEVIN: I meant that when I talk to him, he's a little off.

ANDY: Isn't he a friend of yours?

KEVIN: I've talked to him a few times.

ANDY: When I was over there, he mentioned you more than once.

KEVIN: He did?

ANDY: He mentioned Mike and you.

MIKE: He mentioned me?

ANDY: He said that he was friends with you two.

MIKE: I've talked to him a few times.

ANDY: He said he's friends with you two.

MIKE: All three of us know him pretty well.

ANDY: I can see how you think he's wacky. He is pretty wacky.

MIKE: He goes on those trips to Amsterdam!

ANDY: He was telling me that he goes to Amsterdam for about three weeks, and they just relax at different coffee houses and restaurants.

MIKE: That guy's out of his mind sometimes.

ANDY: He gets something in his head and he just follows it until the end, just to see what's out there. *(To* KEVIN*)* Maybe you should check out some of those open lots over in Eagle Landing.

MIKE: *(To* KEVIN*)* You're looking in Eagle Landing?

KEVIN: I wasn't looking over there.

ANDY: Bill Albee is building his own place up there, and I know the lot next to his, and a few behind it, are still available.

MIKE: Imagine living next to the guy that built your house.

ANDY: Bill Albee does a great job.

MIKE: If you lived next to Bill Albee and you had a problem with something, you could just walk over to his house and tell him all about it.

ANDY: "Hey Bill, my foundation's cracked!"

MIKE: Amazing.

ANDY: "Hey Bill."

MIKE: Yeah.

ANDY: That would never happen though. His foundations are solid, I'm sure.

KEVIN: I wasn't looking in Eagle Landing.

MIKE: That reminds me of another thing I heard. "Living life is what life's about".

KEVIN: That's an obvious statement.

MIKE: Obvious?

KEVIN: That living life is what life's about. It's life, so living it is part of life.

MIKE: I didn't say life was part of life, I said living was what life is all about.

KEVIN: Living life isn't part of life. Living is life.

MIKE: That's what I said.

KEVIN: That's what I'm saying. It's all "life" because it's living. Living is living. It's a stupid statement.

ANDY: A stupid statement?

MIKE: I'm just telling you that I heard it.

ANDY: Mike's not stupid.

KEVIN: I'm not saying Mike's stupid.

ANDY: You both have the same job. If you're saying he's stupid, then you're saying you're stupid, too.

KEVIN: I'm not saying Mike's stupid. I'm saying the statement is stupid.

ANDY: It seems like you think everything Mike says is stupid.

KEVIN: I don't think that.

ANDY: You think we're both idiots.

KEVIN: I do not.

ANDY: I might not be moving into a big new house on a lot in Eagle Landing like you are, but I'm not stupid.

KEVIN: I'm not moving to Eagle Landing.

ANDY: You just said you were looking at lots up there.

KEVIN: I never looked at lots up there.

ANDY: I guess living in Eagle Ridge with Mike and I would be sub-par for you.

KEVIN: No.

ANDY: I guess living next to Mike or living next to me would be sub-par.

KEVIN: Laura and I live in Eagle Hills, where you two *used* to live.

ANDY: When are you moving?

KEVIN: I'm not moving.

ANDY: You're driving around looking at lots every day.

MIKE: You and Laura can't move from Eagle Hills to Eagle Landing.

KEVIN: We're not moving.

ANDY: "Living life is what life's about" seems a little extreme.

MIKE: I guess it is sort of extreme.

KEVIN: What the statement is saying is that if you are living, then you are living.

ANDY: It's saying that getting out there and living is what you should do.

MIKE: That's a little extreme.

ANDY: Monte Gause is out there living. He and his friends are out there living.

KEVIN: We're Monte Gause's friends.

ANDY: We know him.

KEVIN: You just said we were all friends with him.

ANDY: You need to calm down.

KEVIN: Calm down?

ANDY: You're getting mad at me for some reason.

KEVIN: No I'm not. I'm just trying to understand what you're saying.

ANDY: I'm just trying to say that Monte Gause can do certain things in his life that are pretty great.

MIKE: Monte Gause is the one living life.

KEVIN: I'm saying we're all living life.

ANDY: Not in the same way.

KEVIN: Living life is being alive.

ANDY: I'm not living life in the same way. You're not living life in the same way. The three of us are living life in the same ways as each other. Monte Gause is living in different ways.

KEVIN: What different ways?

ANDY: He goes to Amsterdam, Hawaii, Puerto Rico.

MIKE: Puerto Rico?

ANDY: Every other month he goes to Puerto Rico for two weeks.

MIKE: Does he have a place there?

ANDY: He usually stays in the same place every time he goes.

KEVIN: He goes to Puerto Rico every other month for two weeks?

ANDY: Yes.

KEVIN: If he went on vacation as much as you say he does, he'd never be home.

ANDY: Then he's never home.

KEVIN: But he is home. You were just over there.

ANDY: He is home sometimes.

KEVIN: He can't be both never at home and home sometimes.

ANDY: Now *you're* talking extremes.

KEVIN: I'm not talking extremes.

MIKE: What did Monte Gause do in Puerto Rico?

ANDY: He didn't say what he did when he was there.

MIKE: Did he snorkel?

ANDY: He didn't say.

MIKE: I don't think I'd like snorkeling.

ANDY: I think it'd be okay.

MIKE: I can't imagine going underwater and not being able to breathe normally. I can't imagine breathing through that pipe. What if someone were to put something in the pipe? Someone could come by and put something in while you were snorkeling and you'd just go on snorkeling, then you suddenly wouldn't be able to breathe. Maybe someone would put some sort of liquid in your pipe, then you would swallow it and get sick or something. What if you didn't just want to swim on the surface, what if you wanted to swim deeper to get a good look at a fish or a rock or something? I suppose you could scuba dive, but I've heard of people getting the bends, right, the bends? You get the bends and your eyes pop and they get all red with blood, and you get stomach cramps. I hear that then your muscles tighten and you can't swim, and if you're at the bottom of the ocean and you're scuba diving and you get the bends, you're in trouble because you can't move, and you can't see and you're throwing up into your breathing tube. It's like your body explodes. I heard that it's the pressure of all of that water, all of those gallons of water pushing down on you as you swim, and if you're not prepared, then it squashes you like a giant cement block. I can't imagine going into the water and thinking to yourself that might happen to you, how could you get in? You'd have to be thinking whatever the opposite of being squashed is, possibly the feeling of freedom that swimming in a large body of water might give you, but it seems overwhelming to me to even gauge one over the other. I know I'd be thinking, "Giant cement block!" I'd stay on the boat, or better yet, I'd be on the shore. In a chair on shore, or maybe in town.

ANDY: If I were Monte Gause, I'd learn to snorkel.

KEVIN: I'm going home.

MIKE: Don't go home yet.

KEVIN: I'm going home.

ANDY: See you later.

KEVIN: I'm going home or something.

MIKE: Or something?

KEVIN: Or something.

ANDY: You should go home.

KEVIN: I'm going somewhere. I'm doing something.

ANDY: What do you mean you're doing something.

KEVIN: I'm doing something.

ANDY: What are you going to do.

KEVIN: Stop shouting.

ANDY: I'm not shouting.

KEVIN: Stop talking for a second.

ANDY: I can talk if I want.

KEVIN: Be quiet for a second.

ANDY: Don't tell me to be quiet.

KEVIN: Just give me a second to think.

MIKE: Why do you need to think?

KEVIN: Something needs to change.

ANDY: Something?

KEVIN: Something needs to change.

MIKE: Things are great. Don't change things.

KEVIN: Things aren't great.

MIKE: You're great!

KEVIN: *(To* MIKE*)* You aren't great.

ANDY: That's not nice.

KEVIN: *(To* ANDY*)* You aren't either.

MIKE: Andy's great.

KEVIN: None of us are great.

MIKE: All of us are great.

KEVIN: I'm not great.

MIKE: At work?

KEVIN: You said that "Living is the best part of life".

MIKE: I said "Living life is what life's all about". *(To* ANDY*)* Didn't I?

KEVIN: I want to live.

ANDY: Go ahead. Go ahead and move to Eagle Landing. That's what this is about, right? You're moving from Eagle Hills to Eagle Landing, after Mike and I built those houses in Eagle Ridge.

KEVIN: I can't afford to live in Eagle Landing.

ANDY: Anyone can get a loan.

KEVIN: I'm not moving to a different house or a different neighborhood.

ANDY: You're seriously considering it.

KEVIN: No I'm not.

MIKE: You want to change something?

KEVIN: Yes.

MIKE: So do I then.

KEVIN: You can't change something, too.

MIKE: Yes, I can.

KEVIN: I'm going somewhere and you can't come with me.

MIKE: You're going somewhere?

KEVIN: I'm going to go.

MIKE: Where are going?

ANDY: I should go home, too. It's getting late.

KEVIN: I want to leave first. And I'm not going home.

ANDY: We can all leave together, can't we?

KEVIN: I want to leave first. *(He grabs his beer, drinking what is left in one big gulp.)* I'm leaving first.

(KEVIN *exits quickly. A pause.)*

ANDY: Do you need a ride?

MIKE: I've got my car.

ANDY: Does Kevin have his car, too?

MIKE: He rode with me.

ANDY: How's he getting home?

MIKE: Is he walking home?

ANDY: Hm.

(Lights fade to black.)

END ACT ONE

ACT TWO

(Lights up. Four weeks later. The same bar. ANDY *and* MIKE *sit at the table. They have each have a beer and are sharing a basket of pretzels and a cup of mustard.* KEVIN *stands next to the table. He looks like hell.)*

ANDY: Where did you go?

KEVIN: Where did I go?

ANDY: Where have you been? You've been gone for four weeks.

KEVIN: I know.

ANDY: Where did you go?

KEVIN: How are you guys doing?

MIKE: Good.

ANDY: How are we doing?

MIKE: Good.

ANDY: Where did you go?

KEVIN: Can I sit down?

MIKE: Sure.

ANDY: What happened to you?

MIKE: You should call Laura.

KEVIN: Don't tell Laura I'm here, or after tonight that you saw me at all.

ANDY: Why not?

KEVIN: I'm not trying to be sneaky.

ANDY: Sneaky?

KEVIN: Can I sit down with you guys?

MIKE: Do you want a beer?

KEVIN: Okay.

MIKE: Okay.

(MIKE *exits towards the bar. A few beats.*)

ANDY: You look sick.

(*Long pause as* MIKE *gets the beer for* KEVIN.)

(MIKE *enters with a beer. He puts it on the table. A beat as the three look at each other.* MIKE *sits down.* KEVIN *sits down.* KEVIN *sips his beer.*)

KEVIN: Thanks.

MIKE: Where did you go?

KEVIN: I walked around and slept in tall, grassy areas.

ANDY: For four weeks you walked around and slept in tall, grassy areas?

KEVIN: Yes.

MIKE: I thought you went to Canada or out west or something.

ANDY: I thought you left town.

KEVIN: I did leave town.

ANDY: I thought you left town, like out of town for good.

KEVIN: I did.

MIKE: But you came back.

KEVIN: I'm not back to stay.

ANDY: You didn't leave town.

KEVIN: Yes I did.

ANDY: Not for very long.

KEVIN: I've been gone for awhile.

MIKE: *(To* KEVIN*)* You look okay.

ANDY: He looks sick.

MIKE: *(To* KEVIN*)* You look okay to me.

ANDY: What grassy area did you sleep in?

KEVIN: I'm not sure where it was.

ANDY: Where was it?

KEVIN: I'm not sure exactly.

MIKE: Was it north of 17th or did you go past Chris Jamison's?

KEVIN: Four weeks ago I walked out of the door of this bar and I kept walking until I got tired and then I slept then I walked until I got tired and then I slept. I kept doing that until now.

MIKE: You knew where you were, though.

KEVIN: I walked at night and slept during the day so no one would see me walking.

ANDY: No one saw you walking?

KEVIN: No.

ANDY: Someone had to have seen you.

KEVIN: Nobody saw me walking anywhere.

MIKE: But you knew where you were.

KEVIN: I suppose.

MIKE: Where were you?

KEVIN: I walked around in fields and down gravel roads.

MIKE: What did you eat?

KEVIN: I had some money to get food.

ANDY: I thought you didn't see anyone.

KEVIN: I guess I saw the people that I bought food from. I had money in my wallet, and I made it last for a long time.

MIKE: You went to a grocery store?

KEVIN: I went into gas stations.

ANDY: What gas stations?

KEVIN: I went into gas stations and bought food.

MIKE: Are you hungry right now?

KEVIN: No.

MIKE: They still have pretzels here, remember? Pretzels and mustard, too.

ANDY: *(To* MIKE*)* "Remember"? What do you mean "remember"?

MIKE: *(To* KEVIN*)* If you want your old job back, it'll be fine.

KEVIN: I don't want my old job back.

MIKE: It's still available.

KEVIN: I'm not going back to my old job.

MIKE: Your desk is still sitting there.

ANDY: *(To* KEVIN*)* Where have you been?

KEVIN: I walked around and went to convenience stores.

ANDY: Gas stations.

KEVIN: Gas stations. I also was looking around at things. And I drank.

MIKE: You drank?

KEVIN: I drank hard liquor.

MIKE: You walked around drinking hard liquor?

KEVIN: I've been drunk most of the time I've been gone.

MIKE: You're drunk?

KEVIN: I'm not drunk right now, but I was drunk while I was gone.

ANDY: You were drunk for four weeks?

KEVIN: I've been sober today.

MIKE: You were drunk for four weeks straight?

KEVIN: Except for today. *(Pause)* I'm an alcoholic now.

MIKE: You are?

KEVIN: I'm an alcoholic.

ANDY: You're not an alcoholic. You've just been drunk for four weeks.

KEVIN: I didn't know what to do, so I went into a gas station and bought some hard liquor and drank it all. It's hard to remember what happened after that, except that I slept in tall grassy areas and ate food from gas stations, and I slept during the day and walked around at night. Today I wanted to be sober so I could explain a few things and tell you clearly that I'm not coming back again. I know I've been gone a long time. I'm practically unrecognizable.

ANDY: You are not practically unrecognizable.

MIKE: *(To* KEVIN*)* If I saw you walking down the street, I wouldn't think it was you at all. *(Pause)* What did you eat?

KEVIN: Candy and lunch meat.

MIKE: From the gas stations?

KEVIN: Yes.

MIKE: Did you drink sodas?

KEVIN: I just drank hard liquor. Except for today, when I had a soda.

ANDY: Where did you go?

KEVIN: I went into the woods and made a fire and then I went walking around near a lake.

ANDY: I thought you were only in tall, grassy areas.

MIKE: What woods did you stay in?

KEVIN: *(To* MIKE*)* I'm not sure, but they were dense and at night I could hear animals moving around me as I slept.

ANDY: You said that you slept only in the daytime.

MIKE: What kind of animals did you hear?

KEVIN: Deer.

ANDY: What have you really been doing? Were you off at some sort of secret training or something? Were you at some sort of secret business training session for the company you and Mike work for?

MIKE: Our company doesn't have secret business training.

ANDY: How do you know?

MIKE: I would know about any training like that.

ANDY: My company has secret business training trips that it plans for its employees. Word gets out, then everyone knows, but no one talks about it. *(To* KEVIN*)* Were you training for a new promotion?

MIKE: *(To* KEVIN*)* You got a new promotion?

KEVIN: I went out into the woods and drank hard liquor and heard the sounds of deer walking around. I slept in tall, grassy areas during the day, and at night I would walk.

MIKE: You can tell us all about the secret business training.

(Pause)

KEVIN: Two weeks ago I was standing outside of a gas station and I heard the buzzing of a neon sign, and below the buzzing neon sign, on the ground, was a dead bird. The dead bird had its head tucked beside its body so that it looked like it was sleeping.

MIKE: But it was dead?

KEVIN: The buzzing light and the dead bird were connected in something I was hearing and something I was seeing. They were connected by existing in the same moment.

ANDY: Did you want something from us?

KEVIN: When?

ANDY: Did you need something from Mike and I?

KEVIN: I saw new things.

MIKE: What did you see?

KEVIN: Some new things I hadn't ever seen before.

MIKE: Where?

KEVIN: Outside.

MIKE: Outside where?

KEVIN: There's so much to see.

MIKE: What did you see outside?

ANDY: Of course there are things to see outside. I've seen things, too. I went to The Grand Canyon when I was twelve.

MIKE: I haven't been there.

ANDY: It was rocky and windy. I looked across the ledge to the other side. We had some lunch. I bought a comic book.

KEVIN: I'm not saying you haven't seen anything.

ANDY: I'm just telling you where I've been.

KEVIN: I know where you've been.

ANDY: No you don't.

KEVIN: You've been to the same places I've been, except the places I've been to recently.

MIKE: *(To* KEVIN*)* You've been to The Grand Canyon?

KEVIN: Yes.

MIKE: I don't think I've been there.

ANDY: You'd remember going if you'd been there.

MIKE: My family went to some places in the southwest before, so we might have went there.

ANDY: You'd remember The Grand Canyon.

MIKE: I do remember The Grand Canyon.

ANDY: You remember going there?

MIKE: I remember it now.

ANDY: When did you go there?

MIKE: I remember it now.

KEVIN: When I saw the dead bird and the neon sign together I realized is that there are moments like that all over a person's life. There are moments that are like that dead bird and the buzzing sign combining to make a single different experience.

ANDY: I wouldn't call it an experience.

MIKE: How did the dead bird and the neon sign combine?

ANDY: Kevin's been drinking.

MIKE: He's an alcoholic.

KEVIN: That's right.

ANDY: Kevin's been drinking and he doesn't know exactly what he's saying.

KEVIN: I was out in the woods and I met some people.

ANDY: You said you were alone.

KEVIN: I met a man in the woods that said he know of a stream that flowed with a golden light.

MIKE: Did you see get to see the golden light stream?

KEVIN: Yes.

ANDY: I'm calling Laura and she can come pick you up and take you home.

KEVIN: Don't call Laura.

ANDY: I'm calling Laura.

KEVIN: In the stream were rocks that shone and sparkled like jewels.

MIKE: Where is the stream at?

KEVIN: In the woods.

MIKE: Who was the man that showed it to you?

KEVIN: He was a man I met when I was walking around.

MIKE: How did he know about the stream?

KEVIN: He found once it while he was walking in the woods.

MIKE: That's incredible.

ANDY: *(To* KEVIN*)* You were drunk.

KEVIN: Yes.

ANDY: I thought you didn't remember anything.

KEVIN: I really don't know if anything I'm describing actually happened.

ANDY: You don't know if it happened?

KEVIN: I feel like I met a man that knew of a golden stream.

ANDY: You imagined the man and the stream?

KEVIN: I saw it, but I don't know if it was real.

ANDY: So you saw things that weren't real and you're now calling it seeing new things. You were asleep or drunk or blacked out someplace. *(Pause)* You should go home.

KEVIN: I can't.

ANDY: You should go home.

KEVIN: I don't live there anymore.

ANDY: Yes you do.

KEVIN: I saw a dead body. It was lying next to a long, fallen tree and it was wearing a red shirt and jeans. It was curled up by the log, like it was using the side of it for shelter or hugging it for comfort. The body was nearly skeletal and most of its skin was rotted off its face and hands. Its feet were tucked up under its body, but you could see its brown boots. It was covered by tall grass, and I pushed away the tall grass and found the body.

MIKE: Is the body still there?

KEVIN: Probably.

MIKE: Did you tell anyone?

KEVIN: No.

MIKE: Why not?

KEVIN: The body is just one of the things I saw.

ANDY: Or imagined.

MIKE: Where is it?

KEVIN: In the woods.

ANDY: If you saw a body in the woods, then you should tell the police about it.

MIKE: Do you remember where you saw it? Is it near someone's house?

KEVIN: I know who it was.

ANDY: You know who the dead body was?

KEVIN: It was Monte Gause's dead body.

ANDY: No it wasn't.

MIKE: Oh my god.

ANDY: It wasn't Monte Gause.

KEVIN: It was Monte Gause.

ANDY: I saw Monte Gause two days ago.

MIKE: Monte Gause is dead?

KEVIN: It was Monte Gause.

ANDY: It was not.

MIKE: Were you by Monte Gause's house?

ANDY: You were in Eagle Landing?

KEVIN: I was in the woods.

MIKE: There are woods in Eagle Landing.

ANDY: There are trees in Eagle Landing, but I wouldn't call them woods.

MIKE: There's lots of trees down there where it slopes off into the drainage area. (To KEVIN) Were you by the drainage area? It looks like a little waterway, but it's just drainage.

KEVIN: I went back there two days later and it was gone. It was as if there had never been a body there at all. Or a log, or a forest or any tall grass.

MIKE: What was there?

KEVIN: A pond.

MIKE: Maybe the body was swept away by the drainage.

ANDY: And the woods, too? Monte Gause isn't dead. I saw him two days ago.

MIKE: Are you sure it was him?

ANDY: Yes.

MIKE: It was?

ANDY: Yes.

KEVIN: Out in those very same woods, I could see the transparent spirits of the dead.

MIKE: My god.

ANDY: This is too much.

MIKE: *(To* KEVIN*)* Tell us something else.

KEVIN: I saw a large rock near another, larger rock.

ANDY: So what.

MIKE: *(To* KEVIN*)* Two rocks?

ANDY: Everyone's seen two rocks before.

MIKE: You've seen two rocks?

ANDY: Every day.

MIKE: When?

ANDY: Every day.

MIKE: Where?

ANDY: Everywhere.

KEVIN: I also touched the two rocks.

ANDY: Anyone can touch rocks.

KEVIN: I touched a large rock, and then a larger one next to it.

MIKE: *(To* KEVIN*)* What was it like?

ANDY: *(To* KEVIN*)* You should go home to your wife.

KEVIN: I told you that I can't go home.

ANDY: You had all these plans, and you're throwing them all away.

KEVIN: I had no choice.

ANDY: It's not an act of nature. You did it yourself by disappearing into the woods or the tall grass or where ever you went to. You left town for no reason. You were talking about moving to Eagle Ridge over by Mike and me, you were talking about liking your job, you were talking about parasailing.

KEVIN: Everything has changed.

MIKE: *(To* KEVIN*)* You can come back to work.

KEVIN: I have a disease now, and there's nothing I can do.

ANDY: You didn't catch it like a cold.

KEVIN: I'm an alcoholic. I'll never be the same.

ANDY: You're the same now.

KEVIN: I've hit rock bottom.

ANDY: You haven't hit rock bottom.

KEVIN: I have.

MIKE: You can come talk to Ron and I'm sure he'd let you come right back to work. You haven't been gone that long.

KEVIN: I've got problems bigger than either of you can imagine. I've got this disease that I can't control. I've left my old life behind.

MIKE: Maybe we could help you somehow. Maybe it's one of those things where you're reaching out to us.

ANDY: He's not reaching out.

MIKE: Maybe after you get better you can get your life straight and you can get back on track.

KEVIN: Even if I do, and I won't, nothing would be the same. I've got something inside me that's killing me. That can never change.

MIKE: I know—how about Andy and I come with you drinking for a few days? It would be like a party vacation. We could go to different bars and have a few drinks and stay in a motel or something. We could make it fun for you. We could rent some movies and watch a few games or something.

KEVIN: This isn't something that is like that.

MIKE: Why not? It'd be like Marti Gras.

ANDY: I'm not participating in that.

MIKE: Why not?

ANDY: I'm not playing into this mess.

MIKE: It's not a mess.

ANDY: It's a joke, then.

MIKE: *(To* KEVIN*)* Is it a joke?

KEVIN: It's my life. I'm killing myself. Slowly.

ANDY: Why?

KEVIN: I'll be like this for the rest of my life.

ANDY: Why?

KEVIN: Alcoholism.

MIKE: That was really Monte Gause's dead body?

(*Long pause*)

MIKE: (*To* KEVIN) Do you want another beer?

KEVIN: No thanks.

MIKE: (*To* ANDY) Do you want something?

ANDY: I'm okay.

MIKE: Okay.

KEVIN: I want to tell you both about an experience I had.

MIKE: Okay.

KEVIN: It's a sad story, but it's also very amazing.

MIKE: Okay.

KEVIN: I was near a lake, and there was a house near a lake. In the house there was a man, and the man and I had an argument. It was a very large argument, and he and I were very mad at each other. We both were so upset, that the next day we decided to have a duel and fight each other.

MIKE: You had a duel?

KEVIN: The next day, I went back to the house near the lake and the man was there. We each had guns, and we stood together, paced away, and turned and fired our guns at each other. He missed and I shot and killed him. I won the argument.

ANDY: Mike told you that story four weeks ago.

MIKE: It's not the same story. In the story I heard, the two women shot and killed each other. Kevin kills someone in this story, but he's not killed at all.

KEVIN: It happened by a lake.

MIKE: Was this man you shot and killed, was it Monte Gause?

KEVIN: No.

MIKE: There are so many dead people in your stories.

ANDY: Two.

MIKE: There was also that dead bird next to that neon sign.

KEVIN: The amazing part is that the man I shot didn't die. He stood up and smiled at me. He showed me that the guns we had used in the duel weren't real guns and that he was okay. Afterwards, he and I had some lunch and watched television. I learned that outcomes change in every second of our lives. All of us are unsure of outcomes and repercussions until those outcomes and repercussions show themselves in the future. And the future can be one second from now or two years from now—there's no way to know for sure.

ANDY: You are saying that you can't predict what will happen to us. Can't we learn from the experience of others what repercussions may happen, then predict which way things should turn out?

KEVIN: You can't know how things will turn out.

ANDY: I can know that in your "story", what ever happened will have repercussions. If I listen to your story, I learn that I shouldn't be involved in a duel no matter what.

KEVIN: Sometimes you can't predict if you'll be in a duel or not.

ANDY: If I know what I would do in any given situation before it happens, then I know already how I'll respond.

MIKE: How can you be ready for any situation?

ANDY: I may not be ready, but I'll be prepared.

MIKE: What about if something else happens?

ANDY: Like what?

KEVIN: What if your house burns down?

ANDY: No one's house burns down anymore.

MIKE: *(To* KEVIN*)* Kevin saw that forest fire on the news, right?

ANDY: If my house burns down, everyone in my neighborhood's house burns down. The G C, Rory Noble, will be at fault, and I know that he'd never build a house that would burn down.

MIKE: What if someone set it on fire?

ANDY: No one would set my house on fire.

KEVIN: I might.

ANDY: You might set my house on fire?

KEVIN: Someone like me might.

ANDY: What do you mean someone like you?

KEVIN: Someone with lots of problems.

ANDY: You don't have lots of problems.

KEVIN: I do now.

ANDY: No you don't.

KEVIN: I could burn up your house in two seconds, then disappear into the woods forever.

ANDY: Why would you do that?

KEVIN: I'm not going to burn your house, but it doesn't mean someone else won't.

ANDY: We have a neighborhood watch.

MIKE: We do?

ANDY: Yes.

MIKE: What do they do?

ANDY: Look out for each other's houses.

MIKE: Am I supposed to do that?

ANDY: Yes.

MIKE: Are we supposed to walk around checking?

ANDY: Yes.

MIKE: Oh.

ANDY: There's a schedule.

MIKE: There's a schedule?

ANDY: Yes.

MIKE: When do you walk around?

ANDY: We really don't need to walk around.

MIKE: If Kevin's burning up people's houses, we should probably make sure that doesn't happen.

ANDY: He's not burning houses.

MIKE: But he might.

KEVIN: I said someone like me might.

ANDY: Who is "someone like you"?

KEVIN: Someone with lots of problems.

ANDY: It won't happen, and it won't happen to anyone I know.

KEVIN: Yes it has.

ANDY: Who?

MIKE: Oh. Monte Gause?

KEVIN: Yes.

ANDY: You set Monte Gause's house on fire?

KEVIN: I did.

ANDY: His house isn't on fire.

KEVIN: Right now it is.

ANDY: No it's not.

KEVIN: Yes it is.

MIKE: You set Monte Gause's house on fire?

KEVIN: Let's think of the repercussions of his house on fire or his house not on fire.

ANDY: The repercussions?

KEVIN: His house might or might not be ablaze.

MIKE: Maybe we should call Monte and see if he's home.

ANDY: I'm not calling anyone.

MIKE: I'll call him.

ANDY: We're not bothering Monte Gause with any of this.

MIKE: We can hang up if he answers.

ANDY: Kevin wants us to get all worked up and I'm not going to.

KEVIN: Monte Gause's house is on fire.

MIKE: It is?

ANDY: No it's not.

KEVIN: (To MIKE) Your house is on fire.

ANDY: Stop it.

KEVIN: I burned up Mike's house.

ANDY: Stop saying things like that.

KEVIN: It's all gone by now.

ANDY: If you don't shut-up, I'll beat the hell out of you.

KEVIN: Wow.

ANDY: Is Mike's house on fire?

KEVIN: Yes.

ANDY: Is Mike's house on fire?

KEVIN: No.

ANDY: Why are you doing this?

KEVIN: I'm unpredictable and a stranger to you now.

MIKE: You are practically unrecognizable.

KEVIN: Yep.

ANDY: What are you trying to prove?

KEVIN: I want to say goodbye forever.

(Pause)

MIKE: You scared me when you said my house was on fire.

KEVIN: You had a brief knowledge as if everything you own is gone.

MIKE: That's true.

KEVIN: That's my life every moment of every day because everything I once had has disappeared.

ANDY: Then stop what you're doing.

KEVIN: I'm in a pattern I can't stop, and I'll stop when the time is right, and when the time is right, then things will never be the same as they were the moment before or the moment after. Currently, my life is in chaos, but that will work itself out in the long run, but never completely.

ANDY: You'll be dead soon if you keep acting this way.

KEVIN: I think that when death comes, when I'm there on the edge, ready to go over into oblivion, I'll see before me the way back, and turn and start to make my way. But the way back will be more harrowing than the way there. It's a journey that will build character and make me realize what life is all about.

ANDY: You're drinking and stories and messing up you life is all about fixing things that weren't wrong in the first place? You're an alcoholic on purpose?

KEVIN: Maybe at first. Now I'm just an alcoholic. *(Pause)* *(To* MIKE*)* You said you heard that "sleep is the new sex". After I left, that kept going through my mind. "Sleep is the new sex". I couldn't figure out why that statement bothered me so much. Then I realized how both are a certain luxury that some people can't choose one over the other, let alone let one *replace* the other. I didn't want sleep to be the new sex, and I didn't want sleep to be the old sleep and I didn't want sex to be the old sex. I wanted both instead of not having enough time for sex, and sleep being so coveted that it replaces sex in our minds.

(Pause)

MIKE: That was just something I read.

KEVIN: And also, "Living is the best part of life".

MIKE: I said "Living life is what life's all about".

KEVIN: They're the same thing.

ANDY: You purposefully screwed up your life.

KEVIN: I guess so.

MIKE: Is it better now?

KEVIN: I feel different.

MIKE: You do?

KEVIN: It's not the same as before.

MIKE: You can still come back to work.

ANDY: Stop telling him that.

MIKE: I want him to come back to work.

ANDY: Why?

KEVIN: I'm never coming back to work.

MIKE: Where are you going to go?

KEVIN: I have to live in the woods some more and be an alcoholic for a little while longer to know for sure what's going to happen.

ANDY: Or you could go back to your home in Eagle Hills where your wife sits wondering where you are.

KEVIN: I know what I've left behind.

ANDY: You've hurt people.

KEVIN: It's a symptom of the disease.

ANDY: What should we tell Laura?

KEVIN: Don't tell her anything, but if you do talk to her you can tell her that I've become an alcoholic and can't function in society.

ANDY: I'll tell her that you've given up.

KEVIN: I haven't given up, I've given in.

ANDY: Given in to what?

KEVIN: My addiction.

ANDY: You didn't have an addiction before you left! How could you give into something that never had a hold on you before you decided you were going to become an alcoholic?

KEVIN: It wasn't like that. I didn't just decide on a whim to do this.

MIKE: You're fine?

KEVIN: I'm worse, but I'll be better.

MIKE: It's goodbye forever?

KEVIN: That's right.

ANDY: Okay.

KEVIN: Goodbye.

MIKE: Are you going back into the woods? Or the grassy area? Where are you going?

KEVIN: Back outside.

MIKE: What about us? What should we do next?

KEVIN: What did you do while I was gone?

MIKE: I don't know.

KEVIN: You can do that.

MIKE: Okay.

KEVIN: I'll just go.

MIKE: Okay.

KEVIN: I could use a drink.

MIKE: What do you want?

KEVIN: Vodka?

MIKE: Okay. Just a glass of vodka?

KEVIN: Yes.

MIKE: Okay. *(He exits towards the bar.)*

ANDY: Before you left, you were looking in Eagle Landing for a house, weren't you?

KEVIN: No.

(MIKE returns with a glass of vodka. He hands it to KEVIN. MIKE sits at the table.)

(A beat. KEVIN downs the glass of vodka. A beat. KEVIN stands.)

KEVIN: Goodbye. *(Pause. He begins to exit. He pauses, then returns.)* Okay. I've been sleeping next to a transformer in the weeds behind my house in Eagle Hills for four weeks, eating leaves and garbage and drinking water from the neighbor's hose. I've lied to you both tonight and for that I am very sorry. But I am still leaving town, having done something so juvenile and stupid that I could never truly explain why it went on for so long or why I felt the need to lie about it to you both afterwards. It is wholly pathetic to have been sleeping next to a transformer for four weeks, so anything else seemed much better, including becoming an alcoholic. Those things that I told you, the things I saw and experienced, were true stories, but hallucinations born out of terrible hunger and illness. Please tell everyone that asks, including Laura, what I have just said and that I can now go on knowing that everyone will know that I was a scared and selfish man that rather would cower in his backyard than face his own unhappiness, and then lie to his friends about such a sad truth. I have been living alone, hiding behind my house. Nothing could be more pitiable.

ANDY: What?

KEVIN: You can tell everyone that's what happened.

MIKE: That's what really happened?

KEVIN: If you want to, tell people that's what happened. *(A pause. He exits.)*

(A long pause.)

(ANDY stands and exits towards the bar. MIKE sits alone at the table.)

(ANDY returns with two beers. He puts one down in front of MIKE, then sits and puts his down also. A beat. ANDY then raises his glass in a toast. MIKE slowly raises his. They look at each other, take a sip of beer, and put their glasses down.)

(Lights fade to black.)

END OF PLAY